In the Light of Christ

For Brían, Denise, Rónán and Síofra – Easter people

We are in the last night separating us from the dawn after
which there will be no evening; we are at the very entrance
to the nuptial banquet; the Spirit sighs in us for the
moment when the door will open. Therefore we must
watch, with loins girt and lighted lamps in our hands, so
that, at the longed-for moment when the cry will resound,
'Behold the Bridegroom; go out to meet Him', we may
enter with Him and take our place in the company of
Abraham, Isaac, and Jacob. There we shall join all those
who belong to Him and whom he will gather from the
ends of the earth to the messianic banquet: the nuptial
feast prepared by the Father before the creation of the
world, for His Son and the Son's chosen Bride, the Church.

Louis Bouyer, *The Paschal Mystery*
George Allen & Unwin, London 1951

Brian Magee CM

IN THE LIGHT OF CHRIST

The Old Testament Readings
at the Easter Vigil

With commentaries by
Anne F. Kelly, Anne Looney,
Andrew G. McGrady & Donal Neary SJ

VERITAS

First published 1994 by
Veritas Publications
7-8 Lower Abbey Street
Dublin 1

ISBN 1 85390 296 9

The photograph on the cover shows a detail from the sanctuary of the chapel at St Patrick's College, Drumcondra, Dublin.

Cover design: Banahan McManus
Cover photography: Robert Allen
Printed in the Republic of Ireland by Paceprint Ltd

Contents

Introduction   7

Commentary   Brian Magee CM   16

Commentary   Anne F. Kelly   21

Commentary   Anne Looney   28

Commentary   Andrew G. McGrady   36

Commentary   Donal Neary SJ   44

The Easter Vigil Readings in the Roman Lectionary   49

Additional Readings   69

INTRODUCTION

The Easter Triduum

'The greatest mysteries of the Redemption are celebrated yearly by the Church, beginning with the evening Mass of the Lord's Supper on Holy Thursday and continuing until Vespers on Easter Sunday. This time is called the "triduum of the crucified, buried and risen One"; ...during it is celebrated the Paschal mystery, that is the passing of the Lord from this world to his Father. The Church by the celebration of this mystery, through liturgical signs and sacramentals, is united to Christ, her Spouse, in intimate communion' (*Celebrating Easter*, Letter of Congregation for Divine Worship, 1988). This Easter Triduum of Good Friday, Holy Saturday and Easter Sunday is seen as a period in which the faithful are completely devoted to the celebration of what Christ has done for all in his death and rising. The high point of these celebrations is the Easter Vigil, regarded as 'the mother of all vigils'. This night of watching is filled with many powerful symbols, – fire and water, light and darkness, oil and wine, music and words. The words we use are the ancient yet ever-new texts of the Bible.

The foundation of the Easter Vigil

'It must always be borne in mind that the reading of the Word of God is the fundamental element of the Easter Vigil' (*Roman Missal*, Easter Vigil 21). This is the mind of the Church on the night of watching that climaxes the season of Lent and Easter. The Easter Vigil is a time of waiting with the catechumens as they prepare for their initiation; it is a time of prayerful expectation for the celebration of the

Resurrection in the Easter Eucharist. The foundation of that watching and waiting is in the scripture readings that the tradition of the Church puts before us on that night.

These readings are to prepare us for the celebration and renewal of baptismal vows. In union with Christ we imitate his death and rising. We go from death to life, from darkness to light, from captivity to freedom, from the old way of life to the new. In the New Testament reading St Paul will speak of our dying as in the past through our baptism, but our resurrection has still to be won through our upright way of life.

It is fitting that all who celebrate this vigil should know and understand these passages from the Old Testament. They should be the subject of prayer and reflection during Lent and these holy days of the Triduum. This book is seen as a help towards doing that.

How many readings?

The night of watching and waiting for the Easter dawn was from the beginning filled with readings, psalms and prayers. For such a long period of time it is no wonder that the selection and number of readings has varied in the different traditions. The Byzantine rites have had very substantial numbers. The Roman Rite until 1965 had twelve readings. The Lutheran *Book of Worship* still has at least twelve, and the Anglican *Alternative Service Book* gives fourteen.

Today there are nine in the Roman Rite, seven from the Old Testament and two from the New Testament.

It can hardly be argued that the Christian people are not able for this amount of Scripture when these readings are placed before the neophytes, who are just beginning their Christian life and for whom they have profound meaning. All who have the pastoral care of Christian communities should be concerned to help them come to a love of the sacred scriptures.

Unfortunately the rubric in the *Roman Missal* which says that the number of Old Testament readings may be reduced for 'pastoral reasons' has tended to become the normal practice, and the great riches of Scripture have not been made available to congregations in many places. No doubt there may be reasons of available time or security which mean that the Vigil has to be truncated in some circumstances.

A fuller vigil

It is a pity then that this scripture reading is lost to many who celebrate the Vigil each year.

Where a genuine experience of keeping vigil has developed, experience has shown that the appreciation of the Liturgy of the Word has grown. There remains no longer a question of how many readings to leave out, but rather how the Liturgy of the Word can be better celebrated with more time and extra readings. Tradition allows for a choice of other readings that are or have been used. Among these is Ezekiel's story of the dry bones which was in the old Roman Rite and still is in the Orthodox, Lutheran and Anglican rites. It speaks of resurrection and renewal. There is also the baptismal story of Noah and the Flood which was important in the Roman rites. And on this night when we sing, "O happy fault, O necessary sin of Adam, which gained for us so great a Redeemer!' it may be suitable to recall that story in the Book of Genesis. These readings are also provided here as an appendix.

Helping the congregation

Where communities have risked celebrating a full Liturgy of the Word the response has been very positive, and year after year these readings resonate with deeper meaning and grow in the affections of the listeners. Especially where there are catechumens to be initiated will this be so. It cannot happen at once. Work has to be done by all involved to make the Scripture texts accessible.

There are several aids to making this happen.

Firstly there must be a positive approach. The congregation must be encouraged on this night to put aside all clock-watching. This night is different. They must be encouraged to relax. A vigil needs time and space. Space for reflection must be provided.

There is nothing less conducive to this than haste from one item to the next. The readers should not approach the ambo until the commentator has finished. They should not rush the reading. The singers of the Psalms should not be standing ready to start at the first sound of 'This is the word of the Lord', except, of course, at the end of the Exodus reading! And there should be a short pause before the collect is said after the Psalm.

Atmosphere

Then the atmosphere must be conducive to listening – the sound system adequate to the task, the lighting in the church subdued. The tradition is that the Old Testament readings are understood in the light of the Risen Christ, the Paschal Candle being the focus of attention. That tradition is still understood even if some congregations have used the Old Testament readings as a time of preparation for the Service of Light and celebrate in total darkness. This practice allows for the more dedicated to give the time to Vigil, while others may arrive later. If celebrated in darkness, the reader can be lighted and so gain more attention. People then have to listen rather than read along with the reader. It may help the weaker members who need support if visuals such as slides can be provided, whether during, before or after each reading.

Readers

It is obvious that much depends on the readers. The choice and training of readers for this night is based on nothing less than excellence. The variety of literary styles in the texts demands a corresponding variety of voices and proclamation. Voices in dialogue can be used in some of the passages. Some suggestions are given in the readings as printed here. The selection of translations is also important. The versions given here come out of several years' experience, especially in being sensitive to inclusive language.

Sing the Psalms!

It is most important to recognise that with so many words being read there is no alternative but to ensure that the Psalms after the readings are performed musically. People at Christmas Carol services have little problem with many readings because they are placed in the setting of the carols. So the Easter Vigil readings can be seen as set in the context of Psalm-singing. No effort must be spared to make these Vigil Psalms musically attractive. This may mean using adapted versions or alternative versions on occasion. The regulations on church music allow for this, especially for the pastoral reason of full active participation. It should be noted also that some recent arrangements of the readings include musical elements.

Introducing the readings

Finally, people should be helped to meditate on and assimilate the meaning of these scripture passages. The use of a commentator to introduce the readings is allowed for in the rubrics. The work of preparing introductions entails a study of the scripture word, an understanding of the liturgical moment, a sense of the relevance of the texts to the here and now, and feeling for poetic language. These introductions must be well prepared, short and to the point.

Those provided in this book have been created out of the experience of actual Vigils in the past few years. They can be used for the Vigil, or with the Psalms and prayers for private prayer and preparation, and as an example of what can be done in each community as it learns each year to keep this 'night truly blessed when heaven is wedded to earth'.

The pattern of readings on which the commentaries are based is as follows:

1. GENESIS 1:1 - 2:2. ABOUT CREATION

God saw all that he had made, and indeed it was very good.
The understanding of Baptism as our new creation in the image of God makes this first reading appropriate on this night. This is a proclamation to the catechumens and the already baptised of God's creative work at all times.

2. GENESIS 22:1-18. ABOUT ABRAHAM'S SACRIFICE

The sacrifice of Abraham, our father in faith.
The Isaac story has been seen by Christians from the beginnning as a type of Christ's sacrifice. The carrying of the wood represents the cross and his reprieve from death is seen as a kind of resurrection.

3. EXODUS 14:15-15:1. ABOUT THE PASSAGE THROUGH THE RED SEA

The Israelites went on dry ground right through the sea.
This is the most important reading of the night. The crossing of the sea is the type of Christ's death and resurrection, and of the Christian's journey in baptism through dying and rising with Christ.

4. ISAIAH 54:5-14. ABOUT THE NEW JERUSALEM

With everlasting love I will have compassion on you, says the LORD, your Redeemer.
This passage in which Deutero-Isaiah speaks of the return from exile has several pictures. In the Exodus God had taken Israel as a bride, in the Exile he had rejected her but only for a moment; in his compassion he brings her back.

Christ's compassion for his Church is seen in his death and resurrection. The new kingdom is rebuilt with precious stones, the Church shines forth in splendour.

5. ISAIAH 55:1-11. ABOUT SALVATION FREELY OFFERED TO ALL

Incline your ear, and come to me; listen, so that you may live. I will make with you an everlasting covenant.
The Easter Eucharist this night is a foretaste of the eschatological banquet to which all are invited, and to which all Lenten preparation has been directed. This is why God's word has gone out and has not returned empty.

6. BARUCH 3:9-15, 32:1-4. ABOUT THE FOUNTAIN OF WISDOM

Walk towards the shining of her light.
The images of Egyptian captivity and Babylonian exile are used tonight to speak to us of alienation from God. We are called to return to him from the land of our enemies, to enter into the full life of the Church.

7. EZEKIEL 36:16-28. ABOUT A NEW HEART AND A NEW SPIRIT

I shall pour clean water over you and you will be cleansed; I shall give you a new heart, and put a new spirit in you.
Exile was a punishment for Israel's sin; return demands purification, new heart, new spirit. This is achieved for the Christian through Baptism in which new birth and a new spirit are achieved through Christ's death and resurrection.

Additional Readings

GENESIS 3:1-13, 22-24. ABOUT THE FALL OF OUR FIRST PARENTS

The LORD God sent him forth from the garden of Eden.
Tonight we celebrate the new Adam from whom came our redemption from sin. Through his saving work Christ has opened up again the doors of paradise for us.

GENESIS 7:1-5, 10-18, 8:6-18, 9:8-13. ABOUT NOAH AND THE FLOOD

I have set my bow in the clouds, and it shall be a sign of the covenant between me and the earth.
The story of Noah saved through water in the wood of the ark has been seen since early times as a type of baptism – salvation achieved through the water of baptism and the wood of the cross. The number of persons saved is eight, making connection with the Eighth Day of the new creation.

EZEKIEL 37:1-14. ABOUT THE VALLEY OF DRY BONES

I will put my spirit within you, and you shall live.
As in Christ we died so in Christ do we come alive. In baptism his spirit brings us new life. The Church is the renewed people of God.

A COMMENTARY ON
THE READINGS FOR THE
EASTER VIGIL

Brian Magee CM

INTRODUCTION: CHRIST HAS DIED. CHRIST IS RISEN

While our readings this night are mainly from the Hebrew Scriptures they speak to us of Christ, of Christ who died for us and rises in glory.

The prayer with which we conclude each reading points this out for us.

And once again we are reminded that when the Scriptures are proclaimed God speaks to us in the here and now.

These are not figures from the past that we contemplate tonight, but people who have meaning for our lives this holy night.

1. GENESIS 1:1 - 2:2

CHRIST AND THE NEW CREATION

We begin by celebrating the new creation
in the light of the risen Christ.
It is appropriate that we proclaim the wonderful
works of God
who created our world,
and put human beings in a special relationship
with him.

But the victory of Christ is a new creation
and the divine image in humans is restored
   after sin had marred it.
Christ died on the sixth day,
and rested on the Great Sabbath of the Passover,
he rises on the Eighth Day,
the First Day of the New Covenant.
He makes all things new.

1.b. GENESIS 7:1-5,10-18; 8:6-18; 9:8-13

CHRIST, LIFTED UP AS A SIGN

Eight people are saved through the water
by the wood of the Ark that Noah built.
We celebrate on this day called the Eighth Day
the salvation brought to us
by the wood of the cross of Jesus Christ.
We go through the water of baptism,
drowned in its flood
in order to come into the life of that new covenant.
Its sign is not the rainbow
but the triumphant cross
adorned with the jewels of Christ's sacred wounds.

2. GENESIS 22:1-18

CHRIST'S FRUITFUL SACRIFICE

In the death and resurrection of Jesus Christ
a new people is formed,
and the promise made to Abraham
to be the father of many nations
is fulfilled.
In the sacrifice of Isaac
the Church has seen a prefiguring

of the sacrifice of Jesus,
the only begotten Son.
Isaac freely consented to death,
his reprieve was a form of resurrection.
Abraham's action brought benefit
to countless numbers of his descendants.
Christ's action has brought salvation to all

3. Exodus 14:15 - 15:1

RISEN WITH CHRIST

The crossing of the Red Sea
is the supreme type of Christ's action in dying and
    rising.
In Christ we also die through the water of baptism
    and rise to a new life.
We continue on our pilgrim journey led by the
    Light of Christ,
striving to be free from the tyranny of sin and death.

4. Isaiah 54:5-14

ALL THINGS RESTORED IN CHRIST

Three images are used to describe God's
compassionate love for his people
to whom he has given new life.
God has taken Israel back like one who takes back
    the bride he had formerly cast off;
and Christ has come to effect our reconciliation.
Israel was the Ark tossed on the flood until God
    abated his anger:
and Christ who stilled the sea of Galilee brings us
    peace.
        The restoration of Jerusalem,

its Temple rebuilt with precious jewels,
prefigures the new Jerusalem:
the Church built on the cornerstone who is Christ.

5. ISAIAH 55:1-11

CHRIST, THE BREAD OF LIFE

Tonight the Risen Christ is present in his Word,
that goes out bringing life and light.
Tonight he shares the Easter banquet as he offers
   us his Body,
the Bread of Life for which we hunger.
Let us seek him while he may be found;
call upon him while he is near.

6. BARUCH 3:9-15; 32:4-4

CHRIST, ETERNAL WISDOM

We share this night with our beloved catechumens
who are asked to remember
the state they are leaving
and to open themselves to true wisdom of life.
Those who will receive new life
through water and the spirit
will be given a wisdom –
the message of eternal life through Jesus Christ,
   eternal Wisdom.
He is a Light shining in our darkness;
let us walk,
new Christians and old,
towards that shining light.

7. EZEKIEL 36:16-28

THE HEALING CHRIST

Ezekiel sees the Exile as a punishment for Israel's
    sin,
and the return requires an act of purification and a
    new spirit.
So also our alienation from God is healed
through Christ's death and rising,
and requires the pouring of the water of baptism
and the outpouring of the Holy Spirit.
We pray this night for all throughout the world
who are to gain new life in the waters of baptism.

7.b. EZEKIEL 37:1-14

CHRIST, VICTOR OVER DEATH

The Easter symbols that surround us this night
speak of new life.
The spring flowers that scent our church
come to us from the dead earth of winter.
We hear now of the living flesh being put on the
dead bones
and the Spirit that breathes life.
In Jesus Christ, risen from the dead,
all things are made new.
In him we have the pledge of eternal life
when we too pass through the gate of death.

A COMMENTARY ON
THE READINGS FOR THE
EASTER VIGIL

Anne F. Kelly

A COMMUNITY JOURNEYS TO THE SOURCE OF ITS BREATH

Our journey always brings us home.
This homecoming to the truth of our lives
teaches us many things about connections.
A passionate yearning for relationship
   is at the heart of who we are.
Tonight we are invited to restore the lost connections,
to weave again the many threads old and new
that make up the tapestry of our story.
To know a love that takes our breath away.
The journey deepens
and takes us to places we had never dreamed
   yet always dreamed.
The centreing stillness of being intimately loved,
of being held and healed and made whole.
Can we breathe deeply from this new centre?
Intimately known
in a space beyond words
we are centred in our beauty,
our preciousness,
our deep connectedness with all living things....
And we know that this need never end.

1. GENESIS 1:1-2:2

CREATION

First there was darkness.
In the great womb of the earth,
from the warm wet centre the first stirrings of life.
Tonight we remember the place of origins,
the spaces where we were knit together.
The first breath.
The blood that flows in veins
  bursting with new life.
Intimately connected from the very dawn of time .
We are part of all creation.
Our lives flow in great waves of connections with
  all living things.
This we remember and it is good.
And we know we will be sharers
in this ongoing creation of self and world
and in the spaces
we will always find God brooding,
wondering and delighting in the possibilities of
new life.

1.b. GENESIS 7:1-5, 10-18; 8:6-18; 9:8-13

NOAH

So soon this new life is struggling
gasping for breath
we rage with a God who grieved
and cried a great flood.
Shedding tidal tears
from the roots of fractured memory
we too grieve for all we have lost.

Our tears the grief of ages
of all our aching and longing.
How sad we have to be
to see the promise of the rainbow.
Always slow to recognise
we too journey
and wait
our forty days and nights
until our dove sent out
returns with olive branch
and the fine powder
of all our yesterdays
becomes as dust
particles caught up
in rainbow light
our journeys shimmering
in the glow
of an Easter dawn.

2. GENESIS 22:1-18

ABRAHAM

And Sara laughed
as she danced
with the God of possibility.
Would she have died
if she had known
what Abraham had been asked to do
with the child of the promise?
Letting go of all plans
bestowing ourselves to deeper listening
    and centreing
where God will provide.
Breathing quietly and deeply

where caught up in these ancient rhythms
we know that nothing is impossible.

3. EXODUS 14:15-15:1

RED SEA

And you sang to our spirits in our leaving
when we would have preferred the old securities
the fleshpots of Egypt.
You blazed a path we had to follow
nurturing new desires
firing deeper imaginings
and dreaming
your cloud above us.
The breath of a new vision
splitting open the confined spaces
where we had dwelt
for so long
in slavery.
You will always
be part of our leaving
and like Miriam we too
will dance with tambourines
in a breath catching
twirling
whirling
dance of new life.

4. ISAIAH 54:5-14

ALL RESTORED

Called again by
this passionate God

Yearning for relationship
Called to restore
the lost connections
Until we breathe again
with one breath
All living things
In the harmony
of this faithful love
that holds and heals
and makes us whole
Where touch
and tenderness
and infinite care
can make us live again

5. ISAIAH 55:1-11

COME TO THE WATER

Again and again on our journey tonight we come
to water.
This time not the turbulent stormy waters of chaos
and destruction
but the calm, clear waters that will refresh
and nurture and strengthen us.
To the restful waters we bring our tired and parched
spirits.
Drinking deep of the water it will travel to the roots
of our spirit breath.
Its clarity and coolness amazing us once more
as open-mouthed we can only receive,
and be glad.
Bubbling up inside us
it swells to a living spring at the centre of who we
are.

It flows out from us in waves of transformation,
seeding and sprouting
in darkened places that await the breath and touch
of God.

6. BARUCH 3:9-15; 32:4-4

HOLY WISDOM

Tonight we have journeyed long and deep.
Now, at last, our community invites us to meet
lady wisdom, hagia sophia.
We look into her face
as into the face of an ancient grandmother
who has watched the child take its first breath,
steadied its first faltering steps.
Know that it is she who has always lived with us,
journeyed with us.
Feel her strong arms enfold you,
rest in her ancient wisdom.
Gazing into her eyes learn discernment and
    strength.
In the storehouse of her memory there is yet
    so much to learn.
As we journey together deeper into
    that ancient breath
we will learn to walk towards the shining
    of her light.
And our spirits will begin to sing.

7. EZEKIEL 36: 16-28

WATER OF LIFE

Called by the community on this night from
    scatteredness to centreing.

Called home.
For our hearts had indeed turned to stone
   in foreign lands
where we lived rootless and without longing.
Now called home
we are invited to yearn again.
To imagine possibility and newness
where we had previously only known
   decay and death.
Beyond the paralysis of imagination
the new spirit-filled breath pushes its ways
   through crevices
and cracks the pavements with sprouting trees.

7.b. Ezekiel 37: 1-14

Dry Bones

Lost again on the journey, your breath stifled.
Finding ourselves in dry desert places of emptiness
   and desolation.
Before us we sense the void,
the darkness at the centre.
The place where we must stay utterly and terribly
   alone.
It is in the waiting that we will come to know.
For we are tempted to flee this haunting place,
to exchange its bleakness for anything.
But it is the very emptiness,
the darkness itself that we must embrace by staying.
Without knowing why or how we must wait.
Our community on this night urges that we be
   faithful to this long waiting.
Until bones are knitted together again
   and our breath returns.

A COMMENTARY ON
THE READINGS FOR THE
EASTER VIGIL

Anne Looney

To Look, to Watch, to See

Every Liturgy of the Word invites us to listen and respond. But in the Liturgy of the Word of the Easter Vigil we are invited to do more than that. We are invited to look, to watch and to see.

And this invitation is well suited to the Nineties where the visual has greater impact that the spoken: the image, the picture or the video is often more important (and sometimes more memorable) than the poem, the story or the song.

We are invited to look tonight, not just because of the slides which accompany these readings but because each reading calls us to look upon one of the many faces of God.

Since the Triduum began our attention has been focused on the suffering face of God. The Vigil readings ask us to open our eyes to faces of God not always familiar, not always expected, not often captured by the artist or icon-maker.

Our ancestors feared the face of God; they looked down in shame. But our God took on a human face and therefore Christians everywhere can look God, as it were, straight in the face, eye to eye.

And this Easter liturgy is the liturgy of eye-to-eyeness – when the here and the beyond are very close indeed.

1. Genesis 1:1- 2:2

Look then, in this first reading,
on the face of the Lord God captured by the writer
of this story of creation:
an earth face,
a face of balance and equity –
a face that looks on creation and finds in it
   the possibility for good.
We who now stand upon the earth
are called to look on God face-to-face
and account for our stewardship.
Sit, then, and look,
and be thankful,
be in awe.
Open your eyes to how things are
and how they are meant to be.

1.b. Genesis 3:1-13, 22-24

This now is the ancient tale from the Book of Genesis
of the woman, the man and the Big Apple.
It's a story that captures the imagination –
there is the crafty serpent, there is love,
   there is a row,
there are accusations and recriminations.
There is punishment –
all the things that seem to be necessary for a modern
bestseller!
This story is not an invitation to look upon
   the face of God,
in fact, such an invitation is impossible
   by the end of the story.
It is instead a mirror in which we look
   upon our own faces,

the way we are, the choices we make,
the place of truth in our lives,
the very real presence of evil in our world.

On this night when we celebrate the passing from
    darkness to light,
the conquering of sin and death,
we are called to come face-to-face with ourselves
and our claim to be a people of the light.

In a country where darkness always threatens,
at a time when it can appear overwhelming,
let this story bring you face-to-face with yourself,
with the darkness within you and within us all.
Face that darkness
but take courage and comfort in the knowledge
that this is the night when it was conquered
    for ever.

2. GENESIS 22:1-18

In this reading the face of God is something of a
    surprise.
It certainly came as a surprise to Abraham,
called upon to sacrifice his only son.
It wasn't the surprise we might think, however,
for deities of Abraham's day were given to such
    requests.
But Abraham's surprise is nothing compared to the
    undocumented
but easily imagined astonishment of Isaac
when he realises the exact nature of his role in the
    sacrifice.

The biggest surprise of all comes at the end
when Abraham's God shows true colours and
　　reveals a face
that will shine not just on Abraham
but on his descendants
who themselves will shine like the stars.
This is a face that does not turn away from
　　humans' affairs
but offers them blessings beyond dreams.

Look then upon this face of surprises,
for Abraham is our father in faith,
we are the stars of heaven,
we can be truly blessed.

3. EXODUS 14:15-15:1

It is not easy to see eye to eye with the
　　God of Exodus.
We knew where we stood with the Genesis God –
a God of equality, balance and fair play.
But in Exodus we find a God whose face is turned
　　firmly in one direction.
For this is a God who takes sides.
This God faces the Israelites and offers no joy to
　　the Egyptians.

We challenge this face of God to explain why,
forgetting that this is the same God who became
　　powerless,
that this God suffered humiliation and pain,
and was poor and imprisoned.

Look then upon this face of God,
a face that takes sides

and look too on the faces of all those with whom
   God marches today.

4. ISAIAH 54:5-14

This offers us the face of a very male God –
a husband who has rediscovered his love
   for his wife.
Not just a man then,
but a Nineties man,
not afraid to show how he feels,
thinking nothing of declaring everlasting love
   for his wife.

This covenant love is also a power for liberation;
it promises freedom from oppression of all kinds,
from fear and from terror.
This then is the face of God that Christ showed
to the crippled woman in the synagogue,
to the woman at the well of Samaria,
to his mother as he hung upon the cross.
Face this face,
men and women gathered here as
   Christian community.
See in it the fidelity, the hope, the justice
   and true love
which is the foundation of all relationships.

5. ISAIAH 55:1-11

Isaiah is very direct in his invitation to look upon
   the face of God.
If you have faced despair,
if you have faced emptiness,
if you have faced hunger or thirst

then look to the God who is near,
a God who is as water,
flowing in abundance,
bringing life,
making things grow.

But this is a God we have found before –
we have been through the waters of baptism,
we will later this night pass through them again,
we shall rejoice as others among us pass through
    them for the first time.

Look upon this face of God
and be reminded of all that is promised by the
    waters of baptism
and all that the baptised promise
to those who are hungry or thirsty or despairing.

6. BARUCH 3:9-15, 32:4-4

In the Wisdom literature of the Old Testament
we come face to face with an often forgotten face of
God – a female face.
And she is far more than just another pretty face!
She has wisdom, strength and understanding
and she lights the way for others to know God.

Baruch is right when he says that this face of God
    has to be sought out.
It is often hidden, lost, kept safely behind more
    acceptable faces of God.
But as Baruch exhorts the people to turn
    towards her,
he calls on us too to face this face of God –
not as a novelty or a passing trend

but in the realisation that without it, without her,
we will be like Israel in Babylon,
alienated, exiled from one another, divided,
    and in darkness.

Look then upon the wisdom of God.
Marvel at her knowledge; rejoice in her shining
    light.

7. EZEKIEL 36:16-28

In our final reading from the Old Testament it is
    difficult to concentrate
on the face of a God committed to so much activity.
This is a God with hands and feet –
a God who creates and sprinkles and gathers.
It is a God who promises much and delivers on
those promises
with a dramatic declaration of ownership;
the God who looks upon us and calls us 'my
people'.
The God we look upon is 'our God'.

We have looked upon many faces of God.
Look now on the face of the God that knows your
heart, your very spirit.
It is more than a face-to-face meeting.
It is more than a staring straight in the eye.
It is an encounter with the God who loves you.

Take care –
in the face of such love it is difficult to remain silent.
Take care –
in the face of such love it is difficult to remain the
same.

A COMMENTARY ON
THE READINGS FOR THE
EASTER VIGIL

Andrew G. McGrady

The past made present

Tonight we discover who we are by looking at our past made present in memory. We open our family photo album and look at
eight snap-shots
eight readings,
eight ancestors in faith,
eight significant moments in the story of our family,
eight images from the history of our relationship
   with the Divine.

Because these are the stories of our ancestors in faith, they
   are our stories.
They enable us to glimpse the mystery of who we are as
we remember the Passover of the Hebrew people from
   slavery to freedom,
the Passover of our Lord Jesus Christ from death to life,
and our own share in his Passover through the waters of
   our baptism.
This is a night for memory and identity.
Let us open our photo-album and gaze at the first picture.

1. Genesis 1:1-2:2

The Overshadowing Spirit

An image from our forefather Adam and our fore-
mother Eve.
Beginnings.
A looking backwards or
a glimpsing forwards?
A past event
or a continuing reality
or a future fulfilment?

The Spirit of God hovering over the waters
the creative womb from which the universe issues,
waters foretelling the baptismal Passover of
rebirth.

Sixfold – a world of goodness.
Humankind the summit of creation
male and female
separately together
the image of the unseen, all-seeing God,
stewards of the Lord's creation.

1.b. Genesis 7:1-5, 10-18, 8:6-18, 9:8-13

Rainbow Warriors

An image from our ancestor Noah.
A once beautiful universe
destroyed by sin.
Cleansed anew by the overwhelming,
overpowering
liberating
waters of the great flood.

A faithful remnant
– of all creation –
– two of every kind –
saved
by water
and the ark.

A new beginning
a new relationship with a loving,
faithful God.
Rainbow warriors,
at one with all of creation
technology used to preserve and protect
rather than to pillage and destroy.

A new order of right relationships
sealed with the colours of the rainbow,
the promise of a God
who saves all from certain death.

2. Genesis 22:1-18

A Father's Sacrifice

A mountain summit
an altar
the wood for sacrifice.
Our aged ancestor Abraham
and his young son Isaac,
the living, en-fleshed promise of God.
A strange
contradictory image.

The call to surrender
the call to obedience
the call to trusting faith in unseeing love

The raised knife
the moment of deepest darkness
of ultimate despair,
God is present
God reveals
God sustains in life.

A sacrifice of obedient faith is made
not one of human blood.
On the mountain-top
the Lord provides.

Such a Father accepts only
the obedience of his Son
on another mountain-top
to sustain all in life
in his blood.

3. EXODUS 14:15-15:1

RITE OF PASSAGE

An image from our ancestor Moses.
Why is this night different from all other nights?
A question asked
an answer passed on
from generation to generation
from age to age
from faith to faith.

A sea of seeming defeat
a return to slavery.
Impenetrable barrier.
A weak, despairing people,
wallowing in doubt, regretting faith

expecting death, denying life.
A powerful oppressor
armed with technology
and arrogance.
Shall the strong inherit the earth again?

A fragile wind
a presence hovering again
over the waters.
A transformation
a journey from certain death
to liberated life.

By-passing
over-passing
under-passing
rites of passage.
Passing over from slavery to freedom
through the midst of powerless terror.
A God who saves from certain death.

4. ISAIAH 54:5-14

WHISPERS

An image from our ancestor Isaiah.
The whispered conversation of lovers.
God is our husband.
We, an unfaithful wife.

A love that remains faithful
in the face of unfaithfulness
that is not denied
in the face of denial,
that does not reject

when rejected,
that waits, and hopes for the return
of the unloving loved one.

A passionate God
who longs and aches
for the return of the loved one.
A God who promises
my love will never leave you.

5. ISAIAH 55:1-11

COME!

The waters of baptism draw closer now
as rain and snow fall from the heavens
and bestow life on the earth.

Threefold invitation.
to those who thirst
to those who hunger
to those who know not justice,
to those who have not money.

Come
come to the water
you will be refreshed.

Come
come to the Word
your emptiness will be filled.

Come
come to the Lord's table
you will receive good things to eat.

7. Ezekiel 36:16-28

New Heart: New Spirit

A word addressed to captives again in Exile
A word addressed to us
during times of dryness.
A promise to those who are to be baptised.

It is because of our sins that we are exiled
dispersed
far from home.

Has the Lord finally abandoned this faithless
  people?
Has God finally removed the rainbow
  from the sky?
Has the husband finally deserted his
  unloving wife?

No.
Clean water
will be poured over us.
A new heart
a new Spirit
will be given to us.
We shall be God's people
God shall be our Lord.

7.b. Ezekiel 37:1-10

Them bones

An image from our ancestor Ezekiel

A hidden valley
A valley of defeat
a valley of death.
A scattering of dry bones.

An absence of the once hovering Spirit.
An absence of the life-giving water.
A God of the dead
denying
a God of the living.

A promise
a prophecy
a Spirit's breath
a vision
a coming-back-to-fullness-of-life.

A COMMENTARY ON
THE READINGS FOR THE
EASTER VIGIL

Donal Neary SJ

1. GENESIS 1:1-2:2

BEGINNINGS AND ROOTS

Beginnings and roots.
Our roots go back to a garden;
the garden of Eden
with its connotations of Tír na nÓg and
    all being well.
The garden had the right balance of every
    flower and shrub.
And relationships were rooted in harmony.
We'll follow the various changes in these roots,
their uprooting, testing, expansion, entwining,
    re-rooting,
naming them, renewing them –
first, let's listen to the sinking of the roots.
By God, –
the whole world is in his image, and, most of all,
in the creation of man and woman.
That's us!
Our beginnings.
It's a good story and the pictures are good too.

1.b. GENESIS 7:1-5, 10-18; 8:6-18; 9:8-13

UPROOTED

Uprooted;
a flood;
and the roots swam, and the banks were broken.
Beauty was destroyed. But not fully.
God and us –
well, we were drifting apart.
Water flooded and destroyed –
but water always means new growth
the rainbow follows the rain.
New roots, the new covenant.
Or a glimpse of it.

2. GENESIS 22:1-18

TESTING THE ROOTS

Testing the roots;
cut into something and see will it last?
Roots of faith and of relationship with God
    are tested.
The roots tested now are among life's deepest roots,
the bond of father and son.
Roots of life – parent/child –
being cut, being severely tested.
Isn't it true that roots are stronger after cutting?

3. EXODUS 14:15-15:1

EXPANDING YOUR ROOTS

Expanding your roots;
roots dividing; like the sea.

They go many ways – underground
  and overground.
Can grow, can rot.
They can block each other.
And there's war, and hatred, and there's division.
Among divided roots, God can walk and bring
  together
a promise of roots going deeper, forever.
New ground, new waters, new roots.
And then we can sing in praise,
always praise,
only praise for unity in division.
This story meant a lot to Jesus too.

4. ISAIAH 54:5-14

ENTWINING YOUR ROOTS

Entwining your roots;
with God and with others;
images of marriage and friendship,
the other big roots of our lives.
Roots entwining is a rough image
but the reality is gentle, kind,
affectionate,
constant, compassionate.
God folds us into himself.
Invites us to him all the time, bit by bit for years,
till Jesus..........
well, more of Jesus in a while,
but we are looking forward to him.
Compassion, kindness,
all the words of the roots of friendship.

5. Isaiah 55:1-11

Be re-rooted

Be re-rooted;
come back, be re-watered:
in prayer,
in relationships
and some of our pictures for this reading are about
marriage and friendship and people.
And the roots will sing.
If you can imagine that – that's the picture.
Music that is soundless, another name for God.
Nothing can stunt the roots –
snow and rain, all comes from God, goes to God.
A bit like ourselves.
We join creation, the world for a short time,
sink our roots, give some life, and then return.
To our beginnings.
In our end is our beginning.
And the roots sing. That's the difference.
And God will greet us with song.
Then our roots can sing.
Singing his song.

6. Baruch 3:9-15, 32:4-4

Naming some roots

Naming some roots;
wisdom,
strength,
understanding,
gladness,
eternity,

discernment,
making good decisions,
light,
peace.
The roots of faithful life, of love, of God.
Roots growing branches in the law.
We're happy in our roots.

7.b. EZEKIEL 37:1-10

NEW ROOTS

The valley of dead roots.
And they come alive.
And this re-rooting doesn't happen naturally.
Our analogy breaks down
and it's as strange as the reading about dry bones
and fleshy bones.
In Jesus –
and we'll think of him more from now on –
that's where life happens.
And the root is changed
because God enters into roots in a totally new way.
We don't grow naturally into God;
growth, love, faith, all the live roots, are gifts.
Like dead bones jumping around again.
We believe this night that graves will open,
dead men and women –
and all of us –
will dance forever.

THE EASTER VIGIL READINGS
IN THE
ROMAN LECTIONARY

These readings are arranged in sense lines for public reading, and in some cases for use by several voices.
The Psalms are included in the NRSV version for personal reflection, as they will normally be sung in a suitable musical version. The prayers that follow are those in the Roman Missal, except for ones for the additional readings.

1. GENESIS 1:1- 2:2

Arranged for three voices

A reading from the Book of Genesis 1:1-2:2

In the beginning when God created the heavens and the
    earth,
the earth was a formless void
and darkness covered the face of the deep,
while a wind from God swept over the face of the waters.
Then God said,
'Let there be light';
and there was light.
And God saw that the light was good;
and God separated the light from the darkness.
God called the light Day, and the darkness he called Night.
And there was evening and there was morning, the first day.

And God said,
'Let there be a dome in the midst of the waters,
and let it separate the waters from the waters.'

So God made the dome
and separated the waters that were under the dome
from the waters that were above the dome. And it was so.
God called the dome Sky.
And there was evening and there was morning, the second day.

And God said,
'Let the waters under the sky be gathered together into one
    place,
and let the dry land appear.'
And it was so.
God called the dry land Earth,
and the waters that were gathered together he called Seas.
And God saw that it was good.
Then God said,
'Let the earth put forth vegetation:
plants yielding seed,
and fruit trees of every kind on earth that bear fruit with
    the seed in it.'
And it was so.
The earth brought forth vegetation:
plants yielding seed of every kind,
and trees of every kind bearing fruit with the seed in it.
And God saw that it was good.
And there was evening and there was morning, the third day.

And God said,
'Let there be lights in the dome of the sky to separate the
    day from the night;
and let them be for signs and for seasons
    and for days and years,
and let them be lights in the dome of the sky to give light
    upon the earth.'
And it was so.
God made the two great lights –

the greater light to rule the day and the lesser light to rule
the night –
and the stars.
God set them in the dome of the sky to give light upon
the earth,
to rule over the day and over the night,
and to separate the light from the darkness.
And God saw that it was good.
And there was evening and there was morning, the fourth day.

And God said,
'Let the waters bring forth swarms of living creatures,
and let birds fly above the earth across the dome of the
sky.'
So God created the great sea monsters and every living
creature that moves,
of every kind, with which the waters swarm,
and every winged bird of every kind.
And God saw that it was good.
God blessed them, saying,
'Be fruitful and multiply and fill the waters in the seas,
and let birds multiply on the earth.'
And there was evening and there was morning, the fifth day.

And God said,
'Let the earth bring forth living creatures of every kind:
cattle and creeping things and wild animals of the earth
of every kind.'
And it was so.
God made the wild animals of the earth of every kind,
and the cattle of every kind,
and everything that creeps upon the ground of every kind.
And God saw that it was good.

Then God said,
'Let us make humankind in our image,
according to our likeness;
and let them have dominion over the fish of the sea,
and over the birds of the air, and over the cattle,
and over all the wild animals of the earth,
and over every creeping thing that creeps upon the
earth.'

So God created humankind in his image,
in the image of God he created them;
male and female he created them.

God blessed them, and God said to them,
'Be fruitful and multiply,
and fill the earth and subdue it;
and have dominion over the fish of the sea and over the
   birds of the air
and over every living thing that moves upon the earth.'

'See, I have given you every plant yielding seed that is
   upon the face of all the earth,
and every tree with seed in its fruit;
you shall have them for food.
And to every beast of the earth,
and to every bird of the air,
and to everything that creeps on the earth,
everything that has the breath of life,
I have given every green plant for food.'
And it was so.

God saw everything that he had made,
and indeed, it was very good.
And there was evening and there was morning, the sixth day.

Thus the heavens and the earth were finished, and all their
  multitude.
And on the seventh day God finished the work
  that he had done,
and he rested on the seventh day from all the work
  that he had done.

This is the word of the Lord.

2. GENESIS 22:1-18

Arranged for four voices

A reading from the Book of Genesis 22:1-18. NRSV

After these things God tested Abraham. He said to him,

'Abraham!'

And he said,

'Here I am .'

He said,

**'Take your son, your only son Isaac,
whom you love,
and go to the land of Moriah,
and offer him there as a burnt offering on one of the
   mountains
that I shall show you.'**

So Abraham rose early in the morning, saddled his donkey, and took two of his young men with him, and his son, Isaac; he cut the wood for the burnt offering, and set out and went to the place in the distance that God had shown him.
On the third day, Abraham looked up and saw the place far away. Then Abraham said to his young men,
'Stay here with the donkey; the boy and I will go over there; we will worship, and then we will come back to you.'

Abraham took the wood of the burnt offering and laid it on his son Isaac; and he himself carried the fire and the knife. So the two of them walked on together.

Isaac said to his father Abraham,

'Father!'

'Here am I, my son.'

'The fire and the wood are here, but where is the lamb for a burnt offering?'

'God will provide himself the lamb for the burnt offering, my son.'

So the two of them walked on together.

When they came to the place that God had shown him, Abraham built an altar there and laid the wood in order. He bound his son Isaac, and laid him on the altar, on top of the wood.

Then Abraham reached out his hand, and took the knife to kill his son. But the angel of the Lord called to him from heaven, and said:

'Abraham, Abraham!'

'Here I am.'

'Do not lay your hand on the boy or do anything to him; for now I know that you fear God, since you have not withheld your son, your only son, from me.'

And Abraham looked up and saw a ram, caught in a thicket by its horns. Abraham went and took the ram and offered it up as a burnt offering instead of his son.

So Abraham called that place *'The Lord will provide'*; as it is said to this day, *'On the mount of the Lord it shall be provided.'*

And the angel of the Lord called to Abraham a second time from heaven and said:
'By myself I have sworn, says the Lord,
Because you have done this, and have not withheld your son, your only son,
I will indeed bless you,
and I will make your offspring as numerous as the stars of heaven
and as the sand that is on the seashore.
And your offspring shall possess the gate of their enemies,
and by your offspring shall all the nations of the earth bless themselves,
because you have obeyed my voice.'

This is the word of the Lord.

3. Exodus **14:15-15:1**

Arranged for two voices

A reading from the book of Exodus 14:15-15:1. NJB

The Lord said to Moses,
'Why do you cry out to me?
Tell the Israelites to march on.
Your part is to raise your staff and stretch out your hand
    over the sea and divide it,
so that the Israelites can walk through the sea on dry
    ground,
while I, for my part, shall make the Egyptians
    so stubborn
that they will follow them,
and I shall win glory for myself
at the expense of Pharaoh and all his army, chariots and
    horsemen.
And when I have won glory for myself
at the expense of Pharaoh and his chariots and horsemen,
the Egyptians will know that I am the Lord.'

Then the angel of God, who preceded the army of Israel,
    changed station and followed behind them.
The pillar of cloud moved from their front and took
    position behind them.
It came between the army of the Egyptians and the army
    of Israel.
The cloud was dark, and the night passed without the one
drawing any closer to the other the whole night long.

Then Moses stretched out his hand over the sea,
and the Lord drove the sea back with a strong easterly
    wind all night and made the sea into dry land.

The waters were divided and the Israelites went on dry
    ground right through the sea,
with walls of water to right and left of them.

The Egyptians gave chase, and all Pharaoh's horses, chariots and horsemen went into the sea after them. In the
morning watch, the Lord looked down on the army of the
Egyptians from the pillar of fire and cloud and threw the
Egyptian army into confusion. He so clogged their chariot
wheels that they drove on only with difficulty, which
made the Egyptians say,
'Let us flee from Israel, for the Lord is fighting on their side
against the Egyptians.'

Then the Lord said to Moses,
'Stretch out your hand over the sea
and let the waters flow back on the Egyptians
and on their chariots and on their horsemen.'

Moses stretched out his hand over the sea and, as day
    broke, the sea returned to its bed.
The fleeing Egyptians ran straight into it, and the Lord
    overthrew the Egyptians in the middle of the sea.
The returning waters washed right over the chariots and
    horsemen of Pharaoh's entire army,
which had followed the Israelites into the sea; not a single
    one of them was left.

The Israelites, however, had marched through the sea on
dry ground, with walls of water to right and left of them.
That day, the Lord rescued Israel from the clutches of the
Egyptians, and Israel saw the Egyptians lying dead on the
sea-shore.

When Israel saw the mighty deed that the Lord had performed against the Egyptians, the people revered the Lord and put their faith in the Lord and in Moses, his servant.

It was then that Moses and the Israelites sang this song in honour of the Lord:

(Ex 15:1-7, 17-18 NRSV)

R. I will sing to the LORD, for he has triumphed gloriously.

I will sing to the LORD, for he has triumphed
  gloriously;
horse and rider he has thrown into the sea.
The LORD is my strength and my might, and he
  has become my salvation;
this is my God, and I will praise him,
my father's God, and I will exalt him. **R.**

The LORD is a warrior; the LORD is his name.
Pharaoh's chariots and his army he cast into the
  sea;
his picked officers were sunk in the Red Sea.
The floods covered them; they went down into
  the depths like a stone. **R.**

Your right hand, O LORD, glorious in power –
your right hand, O LORD, shattered the enemy.
In the greatness of your majesty you overthrew
  your adversaries. **R.**

You brought them in and planted them on the

mountain of your own possession,
the place, O LORD, that you made your abode,
the sanctuary, O LORD, that your hands have
    established.
The LORD will reign forever and ever. **R.**

4. ISAIAH 54:5-14

A reading from the prophet Isaiah

54:5-14 NRSV

For your Maker is your husband,
the LORD of hosts is his name;
the Holy One of Israel is your Redeemer,
the God of the whole earth he is called.

For the LORD has called you like a wife forsaken
    and grieved in spirit,
like the wife of a man's youth when she is cast off,
    says your God.
For a brief moment I abandoned you, but with great
    compassion I will gather you.
In overflowing wrath for a moment I hid
    my face from you,
but with everlasting love I will have compassion on you,
says the LORD, your Redeemer.

This is like the days of Noah to me:
Just as I swore that the waters of Noah would never again
    go over the earth,
so I have sworn that I will not be angry with you
    and will not rebuke you.
For the mountains may depart and the hills be removed,
but my steadfast love shall not depart from you,
and my covenant of peace shall not be removed,
says the LORD, who has compassion on you.

O afflicted one,
storm-tossed, and not comforted,
I am about to set your stones in antimony,
and lay your foundations with sapphires.
I will make your pinnacles of rubies,
your gates of jewels,

and all your wall of precious stones.
All your children shall be taught by the LORD,
and great shall be the prosperity of your children.
In righteousness you shall be established;
you shall be far from oppression, for you shall not fear;
and from terror, for it shall not come near you.

This is the word of the Lord.

5. Isaiah 55:1-11

A reading from the prophet Isaiah 55:1-11. NRSV

Ho, everyone who thirsts, come to the waters;
   and you that have no money, come, buy and eat!
Come, buy wine and milk without money
   and without price.
Why do you spend your money for that which is not
bread, and your labour for that which does not satisfy?
Listen carefully to me, and eat what is good,
   and delight yourselves in rich food.

Incline your ear, and come to me; listen,
   so that you may live.
I will make with you an everlasting covenant,
   my steadfast, sure love for David.
See, I made him a witness to the peoples, a leader and
   commander for the peoples.
See, you shall call nations that you do not know,
and nations that do not know you shall run to you,
because of the LORD your God, the Holy One of Israel, for
   he has glorified you.

Seek the LORD while he may be found,
call upon him while he is near;
let the wicked forsake their way, and the unrighteous
   their thoughts;
let them return to the LORD, that he may
   have mercy on them,
and to our God, for he will abundantly pardon.

For my thoughts are not your thoughts,
nor are your ways my ways, says the LORD.
For as the heavens are higher than the earth,

so are my ways higher than your ways and my thoughts
than your thoughts.

For as the rain and the snow come down from heaven,
and do not return there until they have watered the earth,
making it bring forth and sprout, giving seed to the sower
and bread to the eater,
so shall my word be that goes out from my mouth;
it shall not return to me empty,
but it shall accomplish that which I purpose,
and succeed in the thing for which I sent it.

This is the word of the Lord.

6. BARUCH 3:9-15, 32:4-4

A reading from the prophet Baruch

3:9-15, 32-37. 4:1-4. NRSV

Hear the commandments of life, O Israel; give ear, and learn wisdom!

Why is it, O Israel, why is it that you are in the land of
   your enemies,
that you are growing old in a foreign country,
that you are defiled with the dead,
that you are counted among those in Hades?

You have forsaken the fountain of wisdom.
If you had walked in the way of God,
    you would be living in peace for ever.

Learn where there is wisdom,
    where there is strength,
    where there is understanding,
    so that you may at the same time discern
    where there is length of days, and life,
    where there is light for the eyes, and peace.

Who has found the place of wisdom?
    And who has entered her storehouses?

But the one who knows all things knows her,
    he found her by his understanding.

The one who prepared the earth for all time
    filled it with four-footed creatures;
the one who sends forth the light, and it goes,
    he called it, and it obeyed him, trembling;

the stars shone in their watches, and were glad;
he called them, and they said, 'Here we are!'
They shone with gladness for him who made
them.

This is our God;
    no other can be compared to him!
He found the whole way to knowledge,
        and gave her to his servant Jacob
        and to Israel whom he loved.

Afterwards she appeared on earth
        and lived with humankind.

She is the book of the commandments of God,
        and the law that endures for ever.
All who hold her fast will live,
        and those who forsake her will die.

Turn, O Jacob, and take her;
        walk towards the shining of her light.
Do not give your glory to another
        or your advantages to an alien people.
Happy are we, O Israel,
        for we know what is pleasing to God.

This is the word of the Lord.

7. EZEKIEL 36:16-28

A reading from the prophet Ezekiel 36: 16-28. NJB

The word of the Lord was addressed to me as follows:

'Son of man, the members of the House of Israel used to
live in their own territory, but they defiled it by their
    conduct and actions.
I then vented my fury on them because of the blood they
shed in the country and the foul idols with which they
    defiled it.
I scattered them among the nations and they were
    dispersed throughout the countries.
I sentenced them as their conduct and actions deserved.
They have profaned my holy name among the nations
where they have gone, so that people say of them:
"These are the people of the Lord; they have been exiled
from his land".
But I have been concerned about my holy name,
which the House of Israel has profaned among the nations
where they have gone.

And so, say to the House of Israel,
        "The Lord says this: I am acting not for your
            sake, House of Israel,
        but for the sake of my holy name,
        which you have profaned among the nations
            where you have gone.
        I am going to display the holiness of my great
            name,
        which has been profaned among the nations,
        which you have profaned among them.
        And the nations will know that I am the Lord –
            declares the Lord –

when in you I display my holiness before their
eyes.
For I shall take you from among the nations
and gather you back from all the countries,
and bring you home to your own country.
I shall pour clean water over you and you will
be cleansed;
I shall cleanse you of all your filth and of all
your foul idols.
I shall give you a new heart, and put a new
spirit in you;
I shall remove the heart of stone from your
bodies
and give you a heart of flesh instead.
I shall put my spirit in you,
and make you keep my laws and respect and
practise my judgements.
You will live in the country which I gave your
ancestors.
You will be my people and I shall be your
God."'

This is the word of the Lord.

ADDITIONAL READINGS

AFTER FIRST READING 1

May be read by several voices

A reading from the Book of Genesis 3:1-13,**22-24**. NRSV

Now the serpent was more crafty than any other wild animal that the LORD God had made.
He said to the woman,

'Did God say, "You shall not eat from any tree in the garden"?'

The woman said to the serpent,

'We may eat of the fruit of the trees in the garden;
but God said, "You shall not eat of the fruit of the tree that is in
the middle of the garden, nor shall you touch it, or you shall
die".'

But the serpent said to the woman,

'You will not die;
for God knows that when you eat of it your eyes will be opened, and you will be like God, knowing good and evil.'

So when the woman saw that the tree was good for food, and that it was a delight to the eyes, and that the tree was to be desired to make one wise, she took of its fruit and ate; and she also gave some to her husband, who was with her, and he ate.

Then the eyes of both were opened, and they knew that they were naked; and they sewed fig leaves together and made loincloths for themselves.

They heard the sound of the LORD God walking in the garden at the time of the evening breeze, and the man and his wife hid themselves from the presence of the LORD God among the trees of the garden.
But the LORD God called to the man, and said to him,

'Where are you?'
He said,

'I heard the sound of you in the garden, and I was afraid, because I was naked; and I hid myself.'

He said,

'Who told you that you were naked? Have you eaten from the tree of which I commanded you not to eat?'

The man said,

'The woman whom you gave to be with me, she gave me fruit from the tree, and I ate.'

Then the LORD God said to the woman,

'What is this that you have done?'

The woman said,

'The serpent tricked me, and I ate.'

Then the LORD God said,
'See, the man has become like one of us, knowing good and evil; and now, he might reach out his hand and take also from the tree of life, and eat, and live forever' –

Therefore the LORD God sent him forth from the garden of Eden, to till the ground from which he was taken.
He drove out the man; and at the east of the garden of Eden he placed the cherubim, and a sword flaming and turning to guard the way to the tree of life.

This is the word of the Lord.

1.b. ADDITIONAL READING

A reading from the Book of Genesis

7:1-5,10-18, 8:6-18, 9:8-13. NRSV

Arranged for two voices

God said to Noah:

I am going to bring a flood of waters on the earth,
to destroy from under heaven all flesh in which is the
   breath of life;
everything that is on the earth shall die.
But I will establish my covenant with you;
and you shall come into the ark,
you, your sons, your wife, and your sons' wives
   with you.
And of every living thing, of all flesh,
you shall bring two of every kind into the ark,
to keep them alive with you;
they shall be male and female.

Of the birds according to their kinds,
and of the animals according to their kinds,
of every creeping thing of the ground according
   to its kind,
two of every kind shall come in to you,
   to keep them alive.

Noah did this; he did all that God commanded him.
In the six hundredth year of Noah's life, in the second month, on the seventeenth day of the month, on that day all the fountains of the great deep burst forth, and the windows of the heavens were opened.
And rain fell on the earth forty days and forty nights.

On the very same day Noah with his sons, Shem and Ham and Japheth, and Noah's wife and the three wives of his sons entered the ark, they and every wild animal of every kind, and all domestic animals of every kind, and every creeping thing that creeps on the earth, and every bird of every kind – every bird, every winged creature.

They went into the ark with Noah, two and two of all flesh in which there was the breath of life. And those that entered, male and female of all flesh, went in as God had commanded him; and the Lord shut him in.

The flood continued forty days on the earth; and the waters increased, and bore up the ark, and it rose high above the earth. The waters swelled and increased greatly on the earth; and the ark floated on the face of the waters.

At the end of forty days Noah opened the window of the ark that he had made, and sent out the raven; and it went to and fro until the waters were dried up from the earth.

Then he sent out a dove from him, to see if the waters had subsided from the face of the ground; but the dove found no place to set its foot, and it returned to him to the ark, for the waters were still on the face of the whole earth.
So he put forth his hand and took it and brought it into the ark with him.

He waited another seven days, and again he sent out the dove from the ark;
and the dove came back to him in the evening,
and there in its beak was a freshly plucked olive leaf;
so Noah knew that the waters had subsided from the earth.
Then he waited another seven days, and sent out the dove;
and it did not return to him any more.

In the six hundred first year, in the first month,
the first day of the month,
the waters were dried up from the earth; and Noah removed the covering of the ark, and looked, and saw that the face of the ground was drying.
Then God said to Noah:
'Go out of the ark, you and your wife,
and your sons and your sons wives with you.
Bring out with you every living thing that is with you of
   all flesh –
birds and animals and every creeping thing that creeps
   on the earth –
so that they may abound on the earth,
and be fruitful and multiply on the earth.'

So Noah went out with his sons and his wife and his sons' wives.
Then God said to Noah and to his sons with him:

As for me,
I am establishing my covenant with you and your
   descendants after you,
and with every living creature that is with you,
the birds, the domestic animals, and every animal of the
   earth with you,
as many as came out of the ark.
I establish my covenant with you,
that never again shall all flesh be cut off by the waters of
   a flood,
and never again shall there be a flood to destroy the
   earth.
And God said;
'This is the sign of the covenant
that I make between me and you
and every living creature that is with you,
for all future generations:
I have set my bow in the clouds,
and it shall be a sign of the covenant between me and the
earth.
When the bow is in the clouds,
I will see it
and remember the everlasting covenant between God
and every living creature
of all flesh that is on the earth.'

This is the word of the Lord.

AFTER SEVENTH READING

Arranged for two voices

A reading from the prophet Ezekiel   37:1-14 NRSV

The hand of the Lord came upon me, and he brought me out by the spirit of the Lord and set me down in the middle of a valley; it was full of bones.
He led me all around them; there were very many lying in the valley, and they were very dry.

He said to me,

'Mortal, can these bones live?'

I answered,
'O Lord God, you know.'

Then he said to me,
'Prophesy to these bones, and say to them:
O dry bones, hear the word of the Lord.
Thus says the Lord GOD to these bones:
I will cause breath to enter you,
and you shall live.
I will lay sinews on you,
and will cause flesh to come upon you,
and cover you with skin,
and put breath in you,
and you shall live;
and you shall know that I am the Lord.'

So I prophesied as I had been commanded;
and as I prophesied, suddenly there was a noise, a rattling,
and the bones came together, bone to its bone.

I looked, and there were sinews on them, and flesh had come upon them, and skin had covered them; but there was no breath in them.

Then he said to me,
'Prophesy to the breath,
prophesy, mortal, and say to the breath:
Thus says the Lord GOD:
Come from the four winds, O breath,
and breathe upon these slain, that they may live.'

I prophesied as he commanded me, and the breath came into them, and they lived, and stood on their feet, a vast multitude.

Then he said to me,
'Mortal, these bones are the whole house of Israel.
They say,
"Our bones are dried up, and our hope is lost;
we are cut off completely."

Therefore prophesy, and say to them,
Thus says the Lord GOD:
I am going to open your graves
and bring you up from your graves, O my people;
and I will bring you back to the land of Israel.
And you shall know that I am the LORD,
when I open your graves,
and bring you up from your graves, O my people.
I will put my spirit within you, and you shall live,
and I will place you on your own soil;
then you shall know that I, the LORD, have spoken and will act' says the LORD.

This is the word of the Lord.